Pocket Books

Ocean Animals

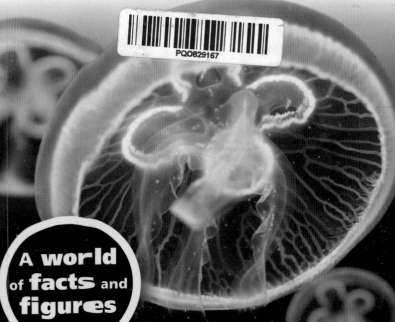

A **world** of **facts** and **figures**

Pocket Books

Ocean Animals

Kane Miller
A DIVISION OF EDC PUBLISHING

First American Edition 2017
Kane Miller, A Division of EDC Publishing

For information contact:
Kane Miller, A Division of EDC Publishing
P.O. Box 470663
Tulsa, OK 74147-0663
www.kanemiller.com
www.edcpub.com
www.usbornebooksandmore.com

Printed and bound in China, January 2019
ISBN: 978-1-61067-594-9   Library of Congress Control Number: 2016941250

Introducing ocean animals

There are around 23,000 vertebrate marine animals and 170,000 invertebrate marine animals, but as ninety-five percent of our oceans are unexplored, there are an estimated nine million more marine animals and plants waiting to be discovered. But for each new animal found, we are nearer to losing more due to fishing, climate change, human development, pollution and shipping accidents.

Over fifty percent of all hawksbill turtle eggs are stolen by humans.

The flamingo tongue snail secretes a liquid that dissolves coral tissue.

A short-beaked common dolphin breaching clear of the water.

Ocean animal characteristics

There is vast diversity in the world of ocean animals.

Some species torpedo through the water or drift on its currents, while others never leave their anchor point. Ocean animals vary in size, from microscopic to huge, and camouflage can mean being blue or gray or colorfully patterned.

But common to all marine animals is breathing air via lungs or gills, feeding, reproducing and being mobile at some stage in their life. Ocean animals are also adapted to cope with water pressure, salt intake and water temperature.

How to use this book

This book gives you the essential facts and informative features on 118 ocean animals, large and small.

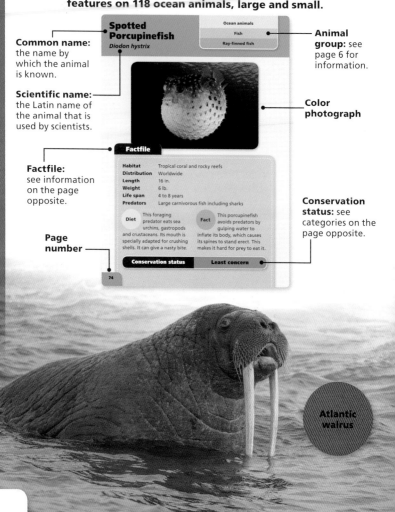

Common name: the name by which the animal is known.

Scientific name: the Latin name of the animal that is used by scientists.

Factfile: see information on the page opposite.

Page number

Spotted Porcupinefish
Diodon hystrix

Ocean animals
Fish
Ray-finned fish

Animal group: see page 6 for information.

Color photograph

Factfile

Habitat	Tropical coral and rocky reefs
Distribution	Worldwide
Length	16 in.
Weight	6 lb.
Life span	4 to 8 years
Predators	Large carnivorous fish including sharks

Diet This foraging predator eats sea urchins, gastropods and crustaceans. Its mouth is specially adapted for crushing shells. It can give a nasty bite.

Fact This porcupinefish avoids predators by gulping water to inflate its body, which causes its spines to stand erect. This makes it hard for prey to eat it.

Conservation status: see categories on the page opposite.

Conservation status   Least concern

74

Atlantic walrus

Factfile

The Factfiles provide six key facts and figures about each animal, from where it lives to what animals eat it.

Habitat
This is the environment in which the animal lives, breeds and hunts.

Distribution
This is the oceans or seas where the animal is found in its natural habitat.

Size, Length or Height and Weight
The animal's dimensions.

Diet
A brief description of the food that the animal hunts and eats.

Migration
This tells if the animal travels for food or to breed.

Clutch size
The number of eggs laid in a nest.

Life span
This is how long the animal lives in the wild. If "in captivity," it is stated.

Predators
This lists the animals that hunt the adult animal. If the young are prey, it is stated. "No natural predators" means the animal is an apex predator.

Fact
Every Factfile comes with an interesting fact about each animal.

Conservation status

Each animal in this book has been given a conservation status. This status indicates the threat of extinction to the species in its native home.

Not evaluated
The animals within this category have not yet been evaluated for their conservation status.

Least concern
This is the lowest risk category. Animals in this category are widespread and abundant.

Near threatened
The animals in this category are likely to become endangered in the near future.

Vulnerable
There is a high risk that animals within this category will become endangered in the wild.

Endangered
There is a high risk that animals within this category will become extinct in the wild.

###
There is an extremely high risk of animals in this category becoming extinct in the wild.

Ocean animal groups

In this book we have divided a selection of ocean animals into four marine vertebrate groups – reptiles, mammals, seabirds and fish – and one wide-ranging invertebrate group.

Reptiles

Of the estimated 10,000 to 12,000 reptile species, only 100 are true marine reptiles: saltwater crocodiles, sea turtles, sea snakes and the unique marine iguana. In the dinosaur age, some reptiles returned to the seas, and despite needing to breathe air, they thrived.

Mammals

There are about 5,000 mammal species of which 119 are marine dwellers. There are five marine mammal groups: whales, dolphins and porpoises; sea cows; sea lions, walruses and seals; otters; and bears. Like all mammals, they have hair or fur, are warm-blooded, breathe air via lungs and have live young.

Birds

There are around 10,000 bird species, which includes roughly 350 birds that rely on a marine environment for all or most of their life. Seabirds and flightless seabirds (penguins) are highly adapted to their habitat. Seabirds live longer and have fewer chicks than their land-based relatives.

Fish

There are 15,300 marine fish species (freshwater fish number about 14,000), but scientists expect there are many more to be discovered. All fish are similar except that marine fish are able to excrete excess salt, while freshwater species are able to retain needed salt.

Ocean sunfish have a rudder, or clavus, instead of a tail fin.

Invertebrates

There are an astounding 170,000 species of marine invertebrates. These animals without a bony internal skeleton (though some have a hard external skeleton) can be found in all oceans from near-freezing to vented water of 752 °F, at all depths and each display amazing survival strategies. They range in size from microscopic plankton to lion's mane jellyfish that have 196 ft. long tentacles.

A crown-of-thorns starfish can eat up to 64 sq. ft. of coral a year.

A colorful peacock mantis shrimp.

Contents

Green Sea Turtle

Chelonia mydas

Factfile

Habitat	Tropical waters
Distribution	Indian, Atlantic and Pacific Oceans
Length	Up to 5 ft. (carapace)
Clutch size	100 to 200 eggs
Life span	Up to 75 years old
Predators	Sharks, orcas

Diet Adults of this species are herbivorous and feed on algae and on shallow-water seagrasses. The juveniles also eat jellyfish, crabs, snails and sponges.

Fact A green sea turtle female only leaves the sea every three to six years in order to nest on the beach she herself was born on. Males never leave the water.

Conservation status   **Endangered**

Hawksbill Turtle

Eretmochelys imbricata

Factfile

Habitat	Tropical reefs, shoals, lagoons
Distribution	Indian, Atlantic and Pacific Oceans
Length	Up to 45 in. (carapace)
Clutch size	Up to 140 eggs
Life span	30 to 50 years
Predators	Humans, sharks, crocodiles, large fish, octopuses

Diet Hawksbill turtles are omnivorous, eating marine algae and other sea plants and mollusks, fish, crustaceans, sponges, marine worms and sea jellies.

Fact These turtles are critically endangered because of human exploitation of their shell, loss of nesting sites and over-predation of eggs and young.

Conservation status   **Critically endangered**

9

Leatherback Sea Turtle

Dermochelys coriacea

Factfile

Habitat	Open seas
Distribution	Worldwide (except polar waters)
Length	Up to 5.5 ft. (carapace)
Clutch size	Up to 110 eggs
Life span	Up to 30 years
Predators	Orcas, sharks

Diet The fragile, scissor-like jaws of this turtle restrict its diet to soft-bodied animals like tunicates and cephalopods (squid), and primarily jellyfish.

Fact The unique leather-like shell (carapace) of this turtle is covered by a thin layer of rubbery skin. Thousands of small bone plates give it its durability.

Conservation status   **Vulnerable**

Loggerhead Sea Turtle

Caretta caretta

Factfile

Habitat	Open oceans, coastal regions, reefs
Distribution	Indian, Atlantic and Pacific Oceans
Length	28 to 37 in. (carapace)
Clutch size	Up to 120 eggs
Life span	30 to 62 years
Predators	Bears, foxes, raccoons, dogs

Diet Loggerheads are carnivorous and their powerful jaws allow them to crush the shells of clams, whelks, horseshoe crabs, mussels and anemones.

Fact The greatest threats to this turtle are predation of the eggs and young by land animals and the loss of nesting sites due to human development.

Conservation status   Vulnerable

Banded Sea Krait

Laticauda colubrina

Factfile

Habitat	Shallow tropical waters off coral islands
Distribution	Eastern Indian Ocean to southwestern Pacific Ocean
Length	35 to 64 in.
Clutch size	4 to 20 eggs
Life span	Unknown
Predators	Sea eagles, sharks

Diet This krait's venomous fangs inject a toxin into its prey, which is mostly eels but also bony fish. The prey is eaten in the water, but digested on land.

Fact To make it easier for this semiaquatic snake to live in water yet still be able to move on land to mate and digest food, its tail is paddle shaped.

Conservation status   **Least concern**

Saltwater Crocodile
Crocodylus porosus

Factfile

Habitat	Marine and brackish swamps, deltas, lagoons
Distribution	Australia, Southeast Asia, India
Length	Up to 20 ft.
Clutch size	40 to 60 eggs
Life span	Up to 70 years
Predators	No natural predators, humans

Diet The diet of this opportunistic predator includes small reptiles and turtles, fish, wading birds, buffaloes, wild pigs, cattle and horses.

Fact The long jaws of this crocodile can exert a pressure of several tons. It ambushes, drowns and swallows its prey whole. Its teeth shred the prey's flesh.

Conservation status   **Least concern**

Marine Iguana

Amblyrhynchus cristatus

Ocean animals

Reptiles

Lizards

Factfile

Habitat	Shallow coastal waters
Distribution	Galápagos Islands
Size	20 to 50 in.
Clutch size	1 to 6 eggs
Life span	5 to 12 years
Predators	Hawks, owls, snakes, crabs, rats, dogs, cats

Diet Most marine iguanas scrape algae from rocks in warm water. Larger iguanas, which retain body heat better, can dive for algae in deeper, cooler waters.

Fact Marine iguanas look a lot like large lizards, but their long tail is taller than it is wide to help propulsion in water. Their blunt noses aid foraging.

Conservation status   **Vulnerable**

Blue Whale

Balaenoptera musculus

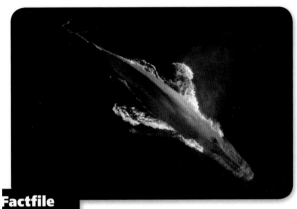

Factfile

Habitat	All open oceans
Distribution	Worldwide (except Arctic waters)
Size	95 to 108 ft.
Weight	165 to 200 tons
Life span	60 to 120 years
Predators	No natural predators

Diet The largest animal to have lived on this planet feeds on one of the world's smallest, krill. An adult can consume forty million shrimplike krill a day.

Fact The blue whale is a deep-sea hunter that comes to the surface to breathe. It can exhale a 40 ft. high column of air vapor through its two blowholes.

Conservation status — **Endangered**

Humpback Whale

Megaptera novaeangliae

Factfile

Habitat	Tropical to polar oceans and seas
Distribution	Arctic, Atlantic and Pacific Oceans
Size	40 to 50 ft.
Weight	25 to 40 tons
Life span	45 to 50 years
Predators	Sharks may feed on sick, injured or young whales

Diet Like the blue whale, this species eats krill. It takes in huge volumes of water with the krill. The krill are trapped in the bristles of the baleen plates.

Fact During its migration, this whale travels over 3,000 miles with barely a rest along the way. This slow-moving whale can cover 1,000 miles in a month.

Conservation status   **Least concern**

Orca
Orcinus orca

Factfile

Habitat	Coastal regions
Distribution	Worldwide
Size	16.5 to 26 ft.
Weight	7.5 to 9.5 tons
Life span	Up to 90 years (female), 60 years (male)
Predators	No natural predators (adults), sharks (young only)

Diet Orcas (killer whales) eat bony fish, sharks, sea lions, elephant seals, octopuses and squid and occasionally narwhal, seabirds and dugongs.

Fact Orcas hold their body upright, head above the water, so they can look for prey. They will create waves that will dislodge seals from floating ice.

Conservation status   **Not evaluated**

Beluga Whale
Delphinapterus leucas

Factfile

Habitat	Inlets, fjords, channels, bays, shallow waters
Distribution	Arctic and subarctic waters
Size	10 to 15 ft.
Weight	1.5 to 1.6 tons
Life span	32 to 40 years
Predators	Orcas, polar bears, humans

Diet The beluga whale will eat almost anything that lives on or near the ocean floor: octopuses, squid, crabs, sandworms and bony fish like flounder.

Fact This whale is known for its vocalization, and its nickname is the "sea canary." It has about eleven sounds, including whistles, squeals, clucks and trills.

Conservation status   **Near threatened**

Sperm Whale

Physeter macrocephalus

Factfile

Habitat	Oceans, especially in deep waters
Distribution	Worldwide (except polar Arctic region)
Size	40 to 42 ft.
Weight	Up to 63 tons
Life span	Up to 70 years
Predators	Orcas

Diet This whale's preferred prey is squid (its body may be scarred by encounters with giant squid), but it will eat octopuses, bony fish, crabs and small sharks.

Fact A sperm whale can dive one to two miles and hold its breath for two hours. But typical dives only last for forty-five minutes and to depths of 1,300 feet.

Conservation status   **Vulnerable**

Narwhal
Monodon monoceros

Factfile

Habitat	Cold open oceans
Distribution	Off the coasts of Canada, Greenland, Norway, Russia
Size	13 to 20 ft.
Weight	0.9 to 1.8 tons
Life span	50 years
Predators	Humans, polar bears, orcas

Diet The diet of the elusive narwhal is squid, Greenland halibut, polar cod, Arctic cod, cuttlefish and shrimp. They suck the prey into their mouth.

Fact All male narwhals possess the long corkscrew tusk, which is actually a canine tooth, that grows throughout their life. Some females grow a tusk.

Conservation status   **Near threatened**

Short-beaked Common Dolphin

Delphinus delphis

Factfile

Habitat	Tropical, subtropical and warm open seas
Distribution	Northeastern Atlantic Ocean, Pacific Ocean
Size	5 to 7 ft.
Weight	220 to 300 lb.
Life span	Up to 20 years
Predators	Large sharks, orcas

Diet Dolphins will seek out schooling fish (like herrings, pilchards, sardines and bonito) and squid and other cephalopods. They eat up to 20 lb. a day.

Fact Pods in excess of 1,000 are common with this intelligent, social, active and vocal species. A sick dolphin will be kept afloat by others in the pod.

Conservation status   **Least concern**

Spinner Dolphin

Stenella longirostris

Ocean animals

Mammals

Whales, dolphins and porpoises

Factfile

Habitat	Tropical high seas, temperate coasts, reefs
Distribution	Pacific, Atlantic and Indian Oceans
Size	4 to 7.5 ft.
Weight	50 to 170 lb.
Life span	20 to 30 years
Predators	Humans, sharks, orcas and other whales

Diet Squid are the bulk of the spinner dolphin's diet, but a group of spinners will hunt at night to depths of 1,000 ft. to herd fish and shrimp into bait balls.

Fact The acrobats of the dolphin world, spinners leap and jump out of the water to perform flips and spins. They also ride the bow waves of boats.

Conservation status   **Data insufficient**

Harbor Porpoise
Phocoena phocoena

Factfile

Habitat	Inshore cold waters, harbors, bays
Distribution	Northern hemisphere oceans
Size	4 to 6.5 ft.
Weight	110 to 200 lb.
Life span	20 years (average)
Predators	Humans, great white sharks, orcas, gray seals

Diet The harbor porpoise has a wide, varied diet that includes mackerel, sand eels, gobies, cod and whiting, and cephalopods and crustaceans.

Fact Harbor porpoise calves are suckled by their mother for four to eight months, and are ready to reproduce four years later. They are a shy and elusive species.

Conservation status   **Least concern**

Dugong
Dugong dugon

Ocean animals

Mammals

Sea cows

Factfile

Habitat	Warm coastal waters, seagrass forests
Distribution	Africa, Asia, Australasia, Red Sea
Size	8 to 10 ft.
Weight	500 to 1,000 lb.
Life span	50 to 70 years
Predators	Sharks, crocodiles, humans

Diet The dugong is also known as the "sea cow" because of its purely herbivorous diet of seagrasses, which it breaks up between its rough lips.

Fact A dugong can remain underwater for up to six minutes before returning to the surface. As it resides in shallow water, it can stand on its tail to breathe.

Conservation status   **Vulnerable**

Florida Manatee

Trichechus manatus latirostris

Factfile

Habitat	Warm, shallow rivers and bays
Distribution	Southeastern North America, northern Central America
Size	8 to 13 ft.
Weight	1,500 to 1,750 lb.
Life span	40 years
Predators	No natural predators, humans

Diet Like their relative, the dugong, manatees are herbivores. They grind seagrasses between molar teeth. New molars are grown to replace worn ones.

Fact Manatees are gentle slow-moving animals. They have no natural predators as they do not compete with sharks and alligators for food.

Conservation status   **Endangered**

Steller Sea Lion

Eumetopias jubatus

Factfile

Habitat	Rocky coasts, offshore islands
Distribution	Northern Pacific Ocean
Size	8 to 10.5 ft.
Weight	.375 to 1.25 tons
Life span	18 (males) or 30 (females) years
Predators	Orcas, great white sharks

Diet These skilled and opportunistic giants of the sea lion world have enormous appetites. They hunt fish, octopuses, squid and sometimes other smaller seals.

Fact Sea lions and fur seals are "eared seals." Unlike true seals, these species have visible ear flaps, long fore flippers and rotating hind flippers.

Conservation status   **Near threatened**

26

Atlantic Walrus

Odobenus rosmarus

Factfile

Habitat	Ice floes, remote rocky coastlines
Distribution	Arctic Circle, North Atlantic Ocean
Size	7 to 11.5 ft.
Weight	.5 to 1.9 tons
Life span	40 to 50 years
Predators	Orcas, polar bears

Diet Using jets of water and its flippers, this walrus forages for bivalves, especially clams, on the sea floor. It literally sucks the meat out of each shell.

Fact This walrus uses its long ivory tusks to anchor it to the ice when its hauls itself from the water, and to attack and puncture predators and rivals.

Conservation status   Not evaluated

Antarctic Fur Seal

Arctocephalus gazella

Ocean animals

Mammals

Sea lions, walruses and seals

Factfile

Habitat	Cold waters, rocky islands, grassy foreshores
Distribution	Antarctic waters, Southern Ocean
Size	4 to 6.5 ft.
Weight	80 (females) to 400 (males) lb.
Life span	15 to 23 years
Predators	Orcas, leopard seals (young only)

Diet Antarctic fur seals swim rapidly in a porpoising fashion and hunt at night for spawning krill, schooling fish, squid and sometimes birds.

Fact In 2000, a six-million-hectare marine park was established on and around Macquarie Island, off New Zealand, to protect populations of this fur seal.

Conservation status   Least concern

Leopard Seal

Hydrurga leptonyx

Factfile

Habitat	Pack ice, cold ocean waters
Distribution	Antarctic region
Size	8 to 10.5 ft.
Weight	450 to 1,300 lb.
Life span	20 to 24 years
Predators	Orcas, sharks, humans

Diet Leopard seals eat penguins, seabirds, small seals, fish, krill and cephalopods (squid, octopuses and cuttlefish). These seals are fierce predators.

Fact Leopard seals are aggressive. They have been known to attack humans in their territory. In response, humans have hunted them in revenge and for sport.

Conservation status   **Least concern**

Southern Elephant Seal

Mirounga leonina

Factfile

Habitat	Rocky island shores
Distribution	Southern Atlantic, Pacific, Indian Oceans
Size	7.5 to 19 ft.
Weight	.5 to 4 tons
Life span	12 to 20 years
Predators	Orcas, leopard seals, sea lions, sharks

Diet Southern elephant seals eat squid and various types of fish, but when these are few, they will dive to great depths (to 3,250 ft.) for small sharks.

Fact During the breeding season, the males are aggressive and fight other males for the right to mate. They make a loud roar from their proboscis.

Conservation status　　　**Least concern**

Sea Otter
Enhydra lutris

Factfile

Habitat	Unpolluted waters close to shore
Distribution	Off the coasts of Russia, North America, Japan
Size	4 to 5 ft.
Weight	30 to 100 lb.
Life span	12 to 15 years
Predators	Sharks, orcas

Diet Sea otters are keystone species. They eat the marine animals – urchins, mussels, snails, abalone and more – that would strip the oceans of kelp.

Fact Sea otters are the second-smallest marine mammal. Instead of a warming layer of blubber they have the densest fur of any animal in the world.

Conservation status **Endangered**

31

Polar Bear

Ursus maritimus

Factfile

Habitat	Coastal fields, floating ice
Distribution	The Arctic
Size	6 to 8 ft.
Weight	330 to 1700 lb.
Life span	20 to 30 years
Predators	Other polar bears, humans

Diet A polar bear can smell a ringed seal, its preferred meal, half a mile away. It will also eat vegetation, geese, bird eggs, small mammals and carcasses.

Fact Polar bears can swim for several hours, covering sixty miles, without resting on an ice floe. Pregnant females will spend autumn and winter on land.

Conservation status   **Vulnerable**

Emperor Penguin
Aptenodytes forsteri

Factfile

Habitat	Open ice, frozen land
Distribution	Antarctica
Height	3.6 to 4.1 ft.
Weight	48 to 82 lb.
Life span	Up to 20 years
Migration	Migrant

Diet These penguins will dive to depths of 1,000 ft. and remain underwater for twenty-two minutes to catch fish, small crustaceans and squid.

Fact One of the perilous times for a penguin pair's single egg is when the male scoops up the egg from the female. If he is too slow, the egg will freeze.

Conservation status　　　　**Near threatened**

Humboldt Penguin

Spheniscus humboldti

Ocean animals

Birds

Flightless seabirds

Factfile

Habitat	Deserts, rocky shores
Distribution	Western South America
Height	22 to 26 in.
Weight	10 to 11 lb.
Life span	15 to 20 years
Migration	Nonmigrant

Diet These penguins will forage for small schooling fish, like anchovies and sardines, for distances up to twenty miles from the breeding colony.

Fact Humboldt penguins can breed twice in a season, each time laying two eggs in burrows or crevices. Many eggs are lost when the nests are flooded.

Conservation status   Vulnerable

Adélie Penguin
Pygoscelis adeliae

Factfile

Habitat	Rocky coasts, ice floes, islands
Distribution	Antarctica
Height	18 to 24 in.
Weight	10 to 11 lb.
Life span	Up to 20 years
Migration	Migrant

Diet Adélie penguins feed primarily on small fish and krill, but their diet also includes cephalopods and crustaceans. They will dive to depths of 575 ft. for food.

Fact Because of their inhospitable habitat, these penguins have no land-based predators. But once in the water, they are hunted by leopard seals.

Conservation status	Near threatened

King Penguin

Aptenodytes patagonicus

Factfile

Habitat	Sparsely vegetated areas
Distribution	Subantarctic islands
Height	33 to 37 in.
Weight	20 to 37.5 lb.
Life span	15 to 20 years
Migration	Migrant

Diet Fish, especially lanternfish, make up almost all the king penguin's diet, but if its preferred meal is not available, it will eat krill and squid.

Fact King penguins have the longest breeding cycle of any bird. A hatchling takes fifteen months to fledge. Chicks are left alone while a parent hunts.

Conservation status   **Least concern**

Laysan Albatross
Phoebastria immutabilis

Factfile

Habitat	Tropical, open oceans; nests on sandy islands
Distribution	Northwestern Hawaiian Islands
Size	31 to 32 in. (length), 76 to 70 in. (wingspan)
Weight	4 to 9 lb.
Life span	12 to 51 years
Migration	Migrant

Diet Laysan albatrosses hunt and feed while sitting on the water. They eat squid, fish, fish eggs, crustaceans and carrion that is discarded from fishing boats.

Fact These birds spend most of their time gliding over the ocean, hardly beating their wings. Dynamic soaring lets them fly vast distances.

Conservation status   **Near threatened**

Southern Giant Petrel

Macronectes giganteus

Factfile

Habitat	Open oceans; nests on islands
Distribution	Antarctica
Size	33 to 40 in. (body), 70 to 79 in. (wingspan)
Weight	7 to 17 lb.
Life span	Up to 25 years
Migration	Migrant

Diet Female southern giant petrels feed on live prey, like krill, squid and fish, whereas marine mammal carrion is the main source of food for males.

Fact These birds have been observed catching seabirds on the wing. They kill or subdue the catch by battering it on the water surface before eating it.

Conservation status   **Least concern**

Brown Pelican

Pelecanus occidentalis

Factfile

Habitat	Coasts, lagoons
Distribution	North, Central and South America, Caribbean
Size	40 to 60 in. (length), 70 to 98 in. (wingspan)
Weight	6 to 12 lb.
Life span	15 to 25 years
Migration	Migrant

Diet A technique this bird uses to catch small fish is to dive from great height, stunning the prey as it strikes and scooping it into its large beak.

Fact Brown pelicans stand on their eggs when incubating. In the 1950s, a pesticide resulted in thin-shelled eggs that cracked, causing a population crisis.

Conservation status	**Least concern**

Blue-footed Booby

Sula nebouxii

Factfile

Habitat	Coasts
Distribution	Central and South America, Galápagos Islands
Size	32 to 34 in. (length), 60 to 62 in. (wingspan)
Weight	2.5 to 4.5 lb.
Life span	Up to 17 years
Migration	Partial migrant

Diet These birds will hunt in groups, flying far out to sea to find schools of small fish. Each bird folds back its wings and plunges into the shoal.

Fact Blue-footed boobies are named for their bright-blue feet and for their clumsy movement on land. Their name comes from a Spanish word for "stupid."

Conservation status   **Least concern**

Northern Gannet
Morus bassanus

Factfile

Habitat	Open oceans; nests on offshore island cliffs
Distribution	North Atlantic Ocean
Size	32 to 43 in. (length), 69 to 71 in. (wingspan)
Weight	5 to 8 lb.
Life span	Up to 35 years
Migration	Migrant

Diet These birds plunge-dive at high speed into shoals of fish or squid. They can hit the water surface at speeds of 60 mph and dive to 10 to 16 feet.

Fact The northern gannet makes its nest on inaccessible cliffs and constructs the nest using mud, grass, seaweed and feathers cemented with excreta.

Conservation status   Least concern

Double-crested Cormorant

Phalacrocorax auritus

Ocean animals

Birds

Seabirds

Factfile

Habitat	Coasts, bays, rivers, mangroves, inland lakes
Distribution	North America
Size	27 to 35 in. (length), 45 to 48 in. (wingspan)
Weight	2.5 to 5.5 lb.
Life span	6 to 8 years
Migration	Migrant

Diet When looking for fish, crabs, eels and more, these birds dive from a floating position on the water, snatch the prey and take it to a ledge to eat.

Fact After a series of dives, double-crested cormorants will perch on piers, ledges, buoys and docks with their glossy black wings spread wide to dry.

Conservation status   Least concern

Common Shag

Phalacrocorax aristotelis

Factfile

Habitat	Coasts; nests on rocky cliffs and islands
Distribution	UK, Norway, Russia, Iceland, southern Europe
Size	27 to 31 in. (length), 37 to 39 in. (wingspan)
Weight	4.5 lb.
Life span	Up to 30 years
Migration	Partial migrant

Diet This shag feeds on fish, mainly sand eels, found on sandy or rocky seabeds. While it will fly distances to find food, it is rarely out of sight of land.

Fact The common shag is a record-breaking diver reaching depths of more than 150 ft. This bird requires only fifteen seconds to rest between each dive.

Conservation status   **Least concern**

Magnificent Frigatebird

Fregata magnificens

Ocean animals

Birds

Seabirds

Factfile

Habitat	Warm water coasts; nests on tree-covered islands
Distribution	USA, Central and South America, Galápagos
Size	35 to 45 in. (length), 85 to 96 in. (wingspan)
Weight	2.5 to 3.5 lb.
Life span	Up to 30 years
Migration	Nonmigrant

Diet When foraging over water, this frigatebird snatches flying fish, squid, jellyfish and crustaceans from just above or on the water. It never swims or dives.

Fact The magnificent frigatebird also hunts over land, taking birds, bird eggs and juvenile turtles from beaches. It will also eat carrion and scraps.

Conservation status   **Least concern**

Oriental Darter
Anhinga melanogaster

Factfile

Habitat	Estuaries, rivers, marshes with trees or bamboos
Distribution	Indian subcontinent, Asia, Southeast Asia
Size	33 to 35 in. (length), 45 to 51 in.
Weight	3.3 to 4 lb.
Life span	9 years
Migration	Partial migrant

Diet This bird will dive, stalk, swim and chase its prey of fish, insects, turtles, snakes, frogs, newts, shrimps and sponges. It will also eat grasses and seeds.

Fact Darters are named for the rapid shooting action they make with their neck to catch fish. This function results from a bend in its neck vertebrae.

Conservation status   **Near threatened**

White-tailed Tropicbird

Phaethon lepturus

Ocean animals

Birds

Seabirds

Factfile

Habitat	Deep tropical oceans; nests on remote islands
Distribution	Pacific, southern Indian and Atlantic Oceans
Size	15 to 16 in. (length), 35 to 37 in. (wingspan)
Weight	8 to 14 oz.
Life span	Up to 16 years
Migration	Migrant

Diet The white-tailed tropicbird will plunge-dive or snatch on the wing flying fish, squid, crabs or snails. It feeds in the morning and early afternoon.

Fact This bird is designed for acrobatic flying. It is streamlined, its long wings are pointed, its tail is wedge-shaped and its bill is angled downward.

Conservation status Least concern

46

Arctic Tern

Sterna paradisaea

Factfile

Habitat	Pack ice; nests in tundra, forests, rocky islands
Distribution	Arctic region, Antarctica
Size	13 to 17 in. (length), 26 to 30 in. (wingspan)
Weight	3 to 4.5 oz.
Life span	15 to 30 years
Migration	Migrant

Diet The tern's diet varies with season and location, but it mostly eats herring and cod, crabs, krill and other crustaceans, and even berries and insects.

Fact A record-breaking migration of 59,650 miles (twice Earth's circumference) was recorded by an Arctic tern between July and November 2015.

Conservation status   **Least concern**

Kelp Gull
Larus dominicanus

Ocean animals

Birds

Seabirds

Factfile

Habitat	Coastal regions; nests on cliffs, islands, roofs
Distribution	Southern hemisphere including Antarctica
Size	22 to 26 in. (length), 50 to 56 in. (wingspan)
Weight	1.1 to 3 lb.
Life span	14 years
Migration	Nonmigrant

Diet The kelp gull hunts and scavenges on a variety of foods. It feeds on live right whales and will also peck a seal pup's eyes and then attack the blinded seal.

Fact To access the meat inside shellfish, kelp gulls will repeatedly drop the shellfish from several feet in the air onto rocks until the shellfish breaks open.

Conservation status   **Least concern**

Atlantic Puffin

Fratercula arctica

Factfile

Habitat	Coasts, open oceans; nests on islands and cliffs
Distribution	North Atlantic and Arctic Oceans
Size	11 to 12 in. (length), 21 to 24 in. (wingspan)
Weight	12 to 16 oz.
Life span	Up to 20 years
Migration	Migrant

Diet Atlantic puffins dive to 200 ft. using their wings to paddle and feet to steer. They hunt sand eels, herring, hake, sprats and occasionally shrimps.

Fact The puffin's colorful beak, which earned the bird its nickname "sea parrot," fades to a gray in winter. The color returns in spring at mating time.

Conservation status   **Vulnerable**

Arctic Skua

Stercorarius parasiticus

Factfile

Habitat	Open oceans; nests on tundra, fells, islands
Distribution	Northern Europe, Asia, northern North America
Size	16 to 18 in. (length), 43 to 49 in. (wingspan)
Weight	12 to 20 oz.
Life span	Up to 32 years
Migration	Migrant

Diet These aggressive birds are known as pirates because they steal most of their food, usually fish, from the beaks of other birds, including puffins.

Fact Arctic skuas spend most of their lives at sea, only coming to land to breed in the Arctic summer. A fledged skua may not touch land for two years.

Conservation status   **Least concern**

50

King Eider

Somateria spectabilis

Factfile

Habitat	Cold coastal shallow waters; nests on tundra
Distribution	Arctic coasts of Europe, Asia, North America
Size	19 to 25 in. (length), 34 to 40 in. (wingspan)
Weight	2.5 to 4.5 lb.
Life span	Up to 18 years
Migration	Migrant

Diet The king eider is a large sea duck and it forages on seabeds to a depth of 82 ft. It feeds on crustaceans, insect larvae, plant matter and mollusks.

Fact During its winter migration, flocks of king eider can number more than 100,000 birds. While breeding, it will forage in freshwater lakes.

Conservation status   **Least concern**

Basking Shark

Cetorhinus maximus

Factfile

Habitat	Coastal warm temperate waters
Distribution	Worldwide
Length	20 to 26 ft.
Weight	5.8 tons
Life span	50 years
Predators	Great white sharks, orcas, humans

Diet These sharks have tiny hooked teeth and gill rakers to filter plankton from the 2,250 tons of water that moves hourly through its 3 ft. wide mouth.

Fact In summer, basking sharks are found near the surface, but in winter they move to depths of 6,250 ft., following their prime source of food, plankton.

Conservation status Vulnerable

Scalloped Hammerhead Shark

Sphyrna lewini

Factfile

Habitat	Warm temperate and tropical waters
Distribution	Atlantic, Indian and Pacific Oceans
Length	12 to 14 ft.
Weight	Up to 335 lb.
Life span	30 years
Predators	Larger sharks (young only)

Diet This shark feeds on sardines, mackerel, herring and sometimes octopuses and other invertebrates. Large species may eat small sharks.

Fact This shark is used in shark fin soup so overfishing has reduced its numbers. Once the fin is cut off, the shark is thrown back in the sea to die.

Conservation status   **Endangered**

Whale Shark

Rhincodon typus

Ocean animals

Fish

Sharks, rays and skates

Factfile

Habitat	Warm tropical open waters
Distribution	Worldwide
Length	36 to 39 ft.
Weight	21 tons
Life span	70 to 100 years
Predators	Blue marlin, blue sharks (young only)

Diet The whale shark is a filter feeder that eats plankton, which includes krill, fish and coral eggs (especially during mass spawnings) and crab larvae.

Fact One female whale shark was pregnant with 300 pups, the largest litter reported for any shark species. Whale sharks don't mature until 30 years of age.

Conservation status   **Vulnerable**

Great White Shark

Carcharodon carcharias

Factfile

Habitat   Cool and temperate coastal and offshore waters
Distribution   Worldwide
Length   Up to 20 ft.
Weight   Up to 2.5 tons
Life span   70 years
Predators   Orcas (infrequently), humans

Diet The great white is the world's largest predatory fish. This efficient hunter feeds on sea lions, seals, turtles and small whales. It will also scavenge.

Fact This feared apex predator swims at speeds of 15 mph and will zero in on its target from below, forcing the prey and itself out of the water.

Conservation status   **Vulnerable**

Blue Shark

Prionace glauca

Factfile

Habitat	Temperate and tropical open waters
Distribution	Worldwide
Length	6 to 11 ft.
Weight	60 to 400 lb.
Life span	Up to 20 years
Predators	Larger sharks (young only)

Diet The blue shark is a predatory and opportunistic hunter. It eats fish, squid and other invertebrates, smaller sharks, seabirds, carrion and garbage.

Fact During mating, the male bites the female, but as her skin is three times thicker than the male's, little or no damage or pain seems to result.

Conservation status   **Near threatened**

56

Tiger Shark

Galeocerdo cuvier

Factfile

Habitat	Tropical and temperate coastal and open waters
Distribution	Worldwide
Length	16 to 20 ft.
Weight	850 to 1,400 lb.
Life span	30 to 40 years
Predators	No natural predators, humans

Diet The tiger shark has a huge appetite and feeds on fish, turtles, sea snakes, seabirds and more. It will also eat carrion, garbage and metal license plates.

Fact Only juveniles bear the black tiger stripes on their upper body. The marks fade as they get older, and on many adults they have disappeared completely.

Conservation status   **Near threatened**

Megamouth Shark

Megachasma pelagios

Factfile

Habitat	Tropical and warm open waters
Distribution	Pacific, Atlantic and Indian Oceans
Length	Up to 18 ft.
Weight	Up to 1,675 lb.
Life span	60 to 100 years (estimated)
Predators	Other large sharks

Diet This shark filter feeds on plankton and jellyfish. Its mouth is edged with photophores. These "lights" may act as lures for plankton and small fish.

Fact This shark was first discovered in 1976, tangled and dead in the sea anchors of a ship. Its name means "huge yawning cavern of the open sea."

Conservation status   **Least concern**

Pelagic Thresher Shark

Alopias pelagicus

Factfile

Habitat	Open warm oceans and seas
Distribution	Indian and Pacific Oceans, Red and Arabian Seas
Length	10 ft.
Weight	155 lb.
Life span	Up to 16 years
Predators	Large sharks, toothed whales

Diet This thresher shark stuns its prey by striking it with its whippy tail. It prefers squid, but it will also eat small fish, crustaceans and seabirds.

Fact Pelagic thresher sharks are solitary, but will hunt with two or three other sharks. They can jump clear of the water making dolphin-like turns.

Conservation status   **Vulnerable**

Shortfin Mako Shark

Isurus oxyrinchus

Ocean animals

Fish

Sharks, rays and skates

Factfile

Habitat	Tropical and temperate waters
Distribution	Worldwide
Length	Up to 13 ft.
Weight	Up to 1,250 lb.
Life span	Up to 32 years
Predators	No natural predators

Diet
The shortfin mako shark is an apex predator. It eats billfish, tuna, mackerel, cod, sea bass and other sharks as well as squid and sea turtles.

Fact
The fastest of all sharks, this mako reaches speeds of 22 mph and can travel 1,250 miles in a month. It can leap twenty feet out of the water.

Conservation status	Vulnerable

Leopard Shark

Stegostoma fasciatum

Factfile

Habitat   Temperate shallow coastal waters
Distribution   Eastern Pacific Ocean
Length   4 to 5 ft.
Weight   40 lb.
Life span   Up to 30 years
Predators   Great white sharks, orcas, dolphins

Diet These sharks track the tide onto mud flats and kelp beds to feed on clams, worms, crabs, shrimp, octopuses, small fish, bat rays and fish eggs.

Fact The silver-bronze leopard shark is easily distinguished by its black spots and markings. Adult species usually have more markings than juveniles.

Conservation status   **Vulnerable**

Giant Manta

Manta birostris

Ocean animals

Fish

Sharks, rays and skates

Factfile

Habitat	Open tropical and temperate waters
Distribution	Worldwide
Width	Up to 23 ft.
Weight	2.2 tons
Life span	50 to 100 years
Predators	Sharks, orcas, humans

Diet Giant mantas are filter feeders that consume thirteen percent of their body weight a week eating shrimp, krill and arrow worms.

Fact Manta rays are regarded as having the largest brain of all known fish species. Scientists record that they employ group feeding behaviors.

Conservation status **Vulnerable**

Cownose Ray

Rhinoptera bonasus

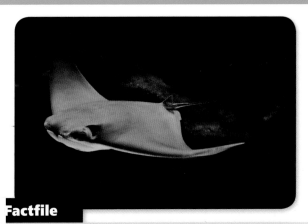

Factfile

Habitat	Tropical and temperate waters
Distribution	Western and eastern Atlantic Ocean
Width	Up to 3.5 ft.
Weight	Up to 35 lb.
Life span	16 to 18 years
Predators	Cobia, sandbar sharks, bull sharks

Diet Cownose rays eat clams, snails, crabs, lobsters and oysters. They forage the seabed, flapping their wings to disturb the sand and reveal their prey.

Fact These rays jump clear of the water and land with splashes and loud noises. It is thought they do this, often in large groups, to show their territory.

Conservation status	Near threatened

Spotted Eagle Ray

Aetobatus narinari

Ocean animals

Fish

Sharks, rays and skates

Factfile

Habitat	Tropical open and coastal waters
Distribution	Worldwide
Width	Up to 10 ft.
Weight	Up to 500 lb.
Life span	4 to 6 years
Predators	Sharks

Diet This ray is a foraging predator that feeds on bivalves, shrimps, crabs, sea worms, octopuses and small fish. Its specialized teeth help it crush hard shells.

Fact The spines on the spotted eagle ray's tail are venomous, and they can inflict serious wounds, but this shy species avoids contact with humans.

Conservation status   Not evaluated

Porcupine Ray
Urogymnus asperrimus

Factfile

Habitat	Tropical inshore waters
Distribution	Eastern Atlantic and Indo-West Pacific Oceans
Width	4 to 5 ft.
Weight	Not recorded
Life span	Up to 21 years
Predators	Sharks, killer whales

Diet This ray forages with its downward-facing mouth on sandy, seagrass and coral seabeds for crustaceans, peanut and annelid worms, and bony fish.

Fact The porcupine ray's upper surface is covered with sharp cone-shaped thorns. Unlike other rays, this ray's long tail lacks a venomous barb.

Conservation status   **Vulnerable**

Broad Skate

Amblyraja badia

Ocean animals

Fish

Sharks, rays and skates

Factfile

Habitat	Open oceans
Distribution	Northeast and eastern central Pacific Ocean
Width	3.3 ft.
Weight	Up to 40 lb.
Life span	Up to 16 years
Predators	Sharks, rays, other skates, gray seals

Diet The broad skate's diet consists of small fish, such as grenadiers, cephalopods and crustaceans that are foraged from rocky shelves and uplifts.

Fact There is little known about this skate, primarily because it is a deepwater ocean species, found at depths in excess of 1,000 feet.

Conservation status   Least concern

Long-nosed Skate

Dipturus oxyrinchus

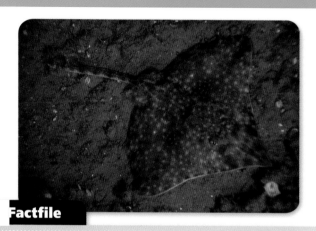

Factfile

Habitat	Sandy or muddy seabeds
Distribution	Eastern Atlantic Ocean, Mediterranean Sea
Width	5 ft.
Weight	160 lb.
Life span	Not recorded
Predators	Sharks, rays, other skates, gray seals

Diet The long-nosed skate skims over sandy and muddy seabeds and feeds on squid and octopuses, crustaceans, such as crabs and shrimp, and bony fish.

Fact The snout on this skate is extremely long and pointed. Like all skates, it has rows of protective spikes on its upper body but no tail barb.

Conservation status   **Near threatened**

Pacific Hagfish

Eptatretus stoutii

Factfile

Habitat   Cold waters
Distribution   North and South Pacific Ocean
Length   12 to 25 in.
Weight   1.8 to 3 lb.
Life span   40 years
Predators   Harbor seals, humans

Diet Hagfish use pairs of rasps on their tongue to hold their prey, which is most often carrion but also includes invertebrates. Males also eat hagfish eggs.

Fact Pacific hagfish have a long, tubular body that they can tie in a knot. They do this to evade a predator, to remove body slime or to get inside a carcass.

Conservation status   **Not evaluated**

Sea Lamprey

Petromyzon marinus

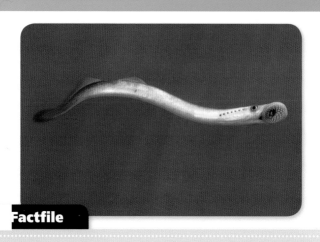

Factfile

Habitat	Open oceans
Distribution	Mediterranean Sea, North Atlantic Ocean
Length	4 ft.
Weight	5.5 lb.
Life span	Up to 8 years
Predators	No natural predators, humans

Diet Lamprey are parasites that suck the blood and body fluids of the host fish. A sucker-like "mouth" fixes them to the host that usually dies.

Fact Sea lamprey migrate from the oceans to freshwater to spawn. The sightless larvae live in soft sediments until they mature after 3 to 4 years.

Conservation status   **Least concern**

Coelacanth
Latimeria species

Factfile

Habitat	Temperate waters
Distribution	Comoro Islands, western Indian Ocean
Length	Up to 6.5 ft.
Weight	200 lb.
Life span	Up to 60 years
Predators	Not recorded

Diet Coelacanth are passive drift feeders, foraging seabeds for cuttlefish, squid, octopuses and bony fish. The hinged mouth allows them to eat large prey.

Fact It was thought that coelacanth were made extinct about 65 million years ago. The first of 1,000 living specimens was discovered in 1938.

Conservation status Critically endangered

Trumpetfish
Aulostomus maculatus

Factfile

Habitat	Tropical reefs and lagoons
Distribution	Western Atlantic Ocean, Caribbean Sea
Length	16 to 32 in.
Weight	3.5 lb.
Life span	Not recorded
Predators	Moray eels, groupers, snapper

Diet These crafty fish "tail" large herbivorous fish and when unsuspecting small fish or shrimp are near, the trumpetfish makes its move.

Fact Trumpetfish have a very long body and they will swim upright, snout down, so they blend in with vertically growing corals and sponges.

Conservation status   **Least concern**

Blue Tang

Paracanthurus hepatus

Factfile

Habitat	Coastal and inshore waters, coral reefs
Distribution	Indo-Pacific Ocean
Length	Up to 15 in.
Weight	1.3 lb.
Life span	8 to 20 years
Predators	Tuna, bar jacks, tiger groupers

Diet The blue tang uses its sharp teeth to tear algae from rocks and corals. In doing so, this colorful herbivore fish helps keep reef systems healthy.

Fact These fish are also known as surgeonfish because of the scalpel-like spines on their tail. The spines extend out when the tang is threatened.

Conservation status   **Least concern**

Banded Butterflyfish
Chaetodon striatus

Factfile

Habitat	Tropical waters, rocky and coral reefs
Distribution	Western Atlantic Ocean
Length	5.5 to 6.5 in.
Weight	Not recorded
Life span	3 to 5 years
Predators	Moray eels, sharks, larger reef fish

Diet This fish is a foraging predator that eats small worms, coral polyps, crustaceans and plankton. It also eats parasites off the body of larger fish.

Fact This butterflyfish's distinctive black stripes confuse its predators. They are unable to tell its head from its tail and in which direction it is moving.

Conservation status   Least concern

Spotted Porcupinefish

Diodon hystrix

Factfile

Habitat	Tropical coral and rocky reefs
Distribution	Worldwide
Length	16 in.
Weight	6 lb.
Life span	4 to 8 years
Predators	Large carnivorous fish including sharks

Diet This foraging predator eats sea urchins, gastropods and crustaceans. Its mouth is specially adapted for crushing shells. It can give a nasty bite.

Fact This porcupinefish avoids predators by gulping water to inflate its body, which causes its spines to stand erect. This makes it hard for prey to eat it.

Conservation status   **Least concern**

Guineafowl Puffer

Arothron meleagris

Factfile

Habitat	Tropical and temperate reefs
Distribution	Indian and Pacific Oceans
Length	20 in.
Weight	Not recorded
Life span	5 to 10 years
Predators	Large carnivorous fish including sharks

Diet This puffer has strong jaws and beak-like teeth to help it dislodge fixed invertebrates, like mussels and barnacles, from their anchor points.

Fact Guineafowl puffers, named for the white spots on black that resemble that of the bird, inflate themselves with water so prey cannot swallow them.

Conservation status   **Least concern**

Leafy Seadragon
Phycodurus eques

Ocean animals

Fish

Ray-finned fish

Factfile

Habitat	Shallow tropical coastal waters
Distribution	Off southern and eastern Australia
Length	Up to 14 in.
Weight	Not recorded
Life span	Up to 10 years
Predators	Fish (young only)

Diet The carnivorous leafy seadragon sucks in its prey – like seahorses, it can't chew food – of small fish, crustaceans, plankton, shrimp and sea lice.

Fact This fish is intricately camouflaged by its color and leaflike fronds resembling seaweed. These help it avoid its predators and ambush its prey.

Conservation status   **Near threatened**

Longsnout Seahorse
Hippocampus reidi

Factfile

Habitat	Reefs, mangroves, seagrass beds
Distribution	Western North Atlantic Ocean, Caribbean Sea
Length	7 in.
Weight	Not recorded
Life span	1 to 4 years
Predators	Few natural predators

Diet This seahorse is an ambush predator. It hides in mangroves, corals and seagrasses and sucks small shrimp, fish and plankton into its toothless snout.

Fact The longsnout seahorse has few predators because it hides itself from danger, has a bony-plated body and has the ability to change color.

Conservation status   Not evaluated

Garibaldi
Hypsypops rubicundus

Ocean animals

Fish

Ray-finned fish

Factfile

Habitat	Bays, exposed rocky shores, kelp forests
Distribution	California coast
Length	11 to 13.5 in.
Weight	Up to 2.2 lb.
Life span	15 years
Predators	Harbor seals, bald eagles

Diet The Garibaldi feeds on sponges, moss animals (bryozoans) and plankton that are found in and around the kelp forests that serve as its home.

Fact These fish are named after Garibaldi, a 19th century Italian leader whose famous army wore bright-red and orange colored uniforms into battle.

Conservation status   **Least concern**

Common Clownfish

Amphiprion ocellaris

Factfile

Habitat	Shallow water coral reefs
Distribution	Eastern Indian and western Pacific Oceans
Length	Up to 4.5 in.
Weight	9 oz.
Life span	Up to 12 years
Predators	Large fish, eels, sharks

Diet The common clownfish feeds on its "host" anemone's parasites, debris and dead tentacles. In return, the anemone affords the fish some protection.

Fact This colorful fish avoids the sting of the anemone tentacles by excreting a mucus that fools the anemone into not stinging. The clownfish is very territorial.

Conservation status   Not evaluated

Bluebanded Goby

Lythrypnus dalli

Ocean animals

Fish

Ray-finned fish

Factfile

Habitat	Coastal waters with rocky seabeds
Distribution	Eastern Pacific Ocean
Length	2.5 in.
Weight	Not reported
Life span	1 to 2 years (in captivity)
Predators	Snapper, grouper, sea bass, flatfish

Diet These fish are carnivorous and have been recorded eating 78 zebra mussels in a day. They aid the recycling of valuable nutrients in reef systems.

Fact Bluebanded gobies are territorial and rarely stray from their hiding places in crevices, under the tentacles of sea urchins or from the seabed.

Conservation status   **Least concern**

Red Lionfish

Pterois volitans

Factfile

Habitat	Tropical waters
Distribution	Indo-Pacific Ocean, western Atlantic Ocean
Length	6 to 12 in.
Weight	Up to 2.5 lb.
Life span	Up to 10 years
Predators	Large bony fish, coastal sharks

Diet This ambush predator remains motionless, waiting for fish to approach, and when they do, it extends its jaw forward, the suction pulling the prey in.

Fact Many of the eighteen long spines on this fish contain a venom that it uses only in defense. It also relies on its colors and fins to deter attacks.

Conservation status   **Not evaluated**

Peacock Flounder

Bothus lunatus

Ocean animals

Fish

Ray-finned fish

Factfile

Habitat	Sandy and rocky seabeds, coral reefs
Distribution	Western Atlantic Ocean
Length	13 to 18 in.
Weight	Not recorded
Life span	3 to 10 years
Predators	Snapper, sharks, rays

Diet The peacock flounder feeds primarily on small fish, even toxic puffers, but it is also known to sometimes prey on crustaceans and octopuses.

Fact This flounder is active during daylight hours and often lies on the seabed, sometimes partially covered by sand, readying itself to ambush its prey.

Conservation status   Least concern

Sarcastic Fringehead
Neoclinus blanchardi

Factfile

Habitat	Rocky temperate reefs
Distribution	Northeastern Pacific Ocean
Length	3 to 12 in.
Weight	Not recorded
Life span	6 years
Predators	Few natural predators

Diet Sarcastic fringehead fish ambush their prey which is thought to include fish, crustaceans and squid eggs. It has a huge mouth and needle-sharp teeth.

Fact This fish, a type of tube blenny, lives in burrows or in the structures of other animals, like snail shells. It will even make its home in a bottle.

Conservation status   **Least concern**

Shaefer's Anglerfish

Sladenia shaefersi

Ocean animals

Fish

Ray-finned fish

Factfile

Habitat	Deepwater sandy or muddy seabeds
Distribution	Western central Atlantic Ocean
Length	Up to 11 in.
Weight	Up to 2.2 lb. (estimated)
Life span	Not recorded
Predators	Few natural predators

Diet Female anglerfish are equipped with a "fishing pole." This luminous lure attracts prey, up to twice the anglerfish's size, that are swallowed whole.

Fact There is little firm information about this highly patterned, deep-sea species as only 10 have been found since it was first discovered in 1976.

Conservation status **Not evaluated**

84

Ocean Sunfish

Mola mola

Factfile

Habitat	Tropical and temperate oceans
Distribution	Atlantic, Pacific, Indian Oceans, Mediterranean Sea
Length	Up to 11 ft.
Weight	Up to 1.1 tons
Life span	82 to 105 years (estimated)
Predators	Orcas (adults), sea lions, marlin (young only)

Diet The ocean sunfish will cover several miles a day hunting down its preferred meal of jellyfish. It will also eat small fish and zooplankton.

Fact This fish looks as though the rear half of its body is missing. It has gritty, rough skin that is covered with mucus. It is the world's heaviest bony fish.

Conservation status   Vulnerable

Red Scorpionfish

Scorpaena scrofa

Factfile

Habitat	Brackish rocky, sandy and muddy seabeds
Distribution	Eastern Atlantic Ocean, Mediterranean and Adriatic Seas
Length	Up to 20 in.
Weight	Up to 6.5 lb.
Life span	10 to 15 years
Predators	Larger fish, sea lions, humans

Diet
Red scorpionfish ambush their prey of fish, crustaceans and mollusks. They lie motionless, camouflaged on rocky seabeds, to wait for a meal.

Fact
This blotchy-pink or red venomous fish has a sharp 12-spined dorsal fin. The fin is fed venom, which is stored under the skin, via channels in the spines.

Conservation status   **Least concern**

Spotted Lanternfish

Myctophum punctatum

Factfile

Habitat	Open oceans
Distribution	Northeastern Atlantic Ocean, Mediterranean Sea
Length	4.2 in.
Weight	Not recorded
Life span	3 years (estimated)
Predators	Larger fish, seabirds, seals, whales

Diet Lanternfish are carnivores that feed on shrimp, fish eggs, fish larvae and small crustaceans. They migrate to shallow water at night.

Fact These fish have photophores – light organs – on their head and body. At dusk, these low lights may confuse predators at deeper depths.

Conservation status   **Least concern**

Scarlet Frogfish

Antennatus coccineus

Ocean animals

Fish

Ray-finned fish

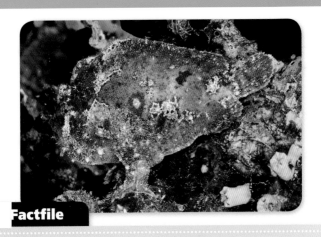

Factfile

Habitat	Intertidal areas, shallow reefs
Distribution	Indian and southern Pacific Oceans, Red Sea
Size	Up to 15 in.
Weight	Up to 2.2 lb. (estimated)
Life span	Not recorded
Predators	Other frogfish, moray eels

Diet Named for its huge mouth that opens to body width, the frogfish ambushes fish and crustaceans attracted by the moving lure on its forehead.

Fact Scarlet frogfish use many camouflage devices to mimic and conceal, including coloring, changing color, appendages and body texture.

Conservation status   Not evaluated

Common Fangtooth

Anoplogaster cornuta

Factfile

Habitat	Deep tropical and temperate oceans
Distribution	Worldwide
Length	Up to 7 in.
Weight	Not recorded
Life span	Not recorded
Predators	Marlin, tuna

Diet Fish and crustaceans are the preferred prey of this species. It opens its mouth and sucks in the prey, which is snagged or trapped in its sharp teeth.

Fact This fish, nicknamed the "ogrefish," has the largest teeth relative to its size. When the mouth is closed, the lower teeth slot into grooves in the upper jaw.

Conservation status   **Least concern**

Black Swallower

Chiasmodon niger

Ocean animals

Fish

Ray-finned fish

Factfile

Habitat	Deep tropical and subtropical waters
Distribution	Worldwide
Length	Up to 10 in.
Weight	Not recorded
Life span	Not recorded
Predators	Long-snouted lancetfish

Diet This fish swallows prey much larger than itself. It grips its prey's tail in its teeth, then gradually takes the prey whole into its expandable stomach.

Fact Many of the black swallowers studied by scientists died. They ate prey ten times their size that rotted in their gut, causing them to explode.

Conservation status   **Least concern**

Elongated Bristlemouth

Gonostoma elongata

Factfile

Habitat	Deep tropical and subtropical waters
Distribution	Worldwide
Length	6.5 to 10.5 in.
Weight	Not recorded
Life span	Up to 2 years
Predators	Fraser's dolphin, tuna

Diet This fish, which has bristlelike teeth, eats zooplankton like seed shrimp, and small crustaceans that are attracted to light-producing cells on its body.

Fact Bristlemouths are regarded as the most abundant vertebrate in the world. They number in the hundreds of trillions to hundreds of quadrillions.

Conservation status   **Least concern**

Spotted Moray Eel

Gymnothorax moringa

Ocean animals
Fish
Ray-finned fish

Factfile

Habitat	Tropical water coral reefs
Distribution	Western Atlantic, Gulf of Mexico, Caribbean Sea
Length	Up to 6.5 ft.
Weight	Up to 5.5 lb.
Life span	10 to 30 years
Predators	Other moray eels, large grouper, barracudas

Diet The spotted moray eel, a poor swimmer, will lie in wait in a crevice, only its head visible, until fish, squid, octopuses, crabs or cuttlefish come near.

Fact This moray eel has been recorded as being aggressive to humans. Its bite is dangerous due to toxins and the pull-back nature of the eel's bite.

Conservation status	Least concern

Giant Moray Eel

Gymnothorax griseus

Factfile

Habitat	Tropical and temperate lagoons and reefs
Distribution	Indo-Pacific region
Length	Up to 10 ft.
Weight	Up to 66 lb.
Life span	3 to 36 years
Predators	Grouper, barracuda, sharks, sea snakes, humans

Diet Giant moray eels are carnivorous, eating other eels as well as cephalopods, mollusks and crustaceans. They will often hunt with coral grouper.

Fact This eel, in common with all moray eels, has very poor eyesight, so it relies on a highly developed sense of smell to find and catch prey.

Conservation status   **Not evaluated**

Brown Garden Eel

Heteroconger halis

Ocean animals

Fish

Ray-finned fish

Factfile

Habitat	Sandy seabeds near coral reefs
Distribution	Eastern Atlantic, Caribbean Sea, Gulf of Mexico
Length	Up to 20 in.
Weight	Up to 2 oz. (estimated)
Life span	Up to 20 years (estimated)
Predators	Pacific snake eels, triggerfish

Diet The brown eel lives in colonies. During the day it can be seen half protruding from its burrow, its mouth open, catching plankton and detritus drifting by.

Fact When threatened or alarmed, every member of a garden eel colony will retreat speedily down into its burrow. These eels never leave the seabed.

Conservation status **Least concern**

94

Broadclub Cuttlefish

Sepia latimanus

Factfile

Habitat	Tropical to temperate coral reefs
Distribution	Indian and western Pacific Oceans
Length	Up to 20 in. (mantle only)
Weight	48.5 lb.
Life span	Up to 2 years
Predators	Large fish, sharks, other cuttlefish

Diet This cuttlefish uses broad pads on the ends of its feeding tentacles to capture fish and invertebrates. The tentacles take the prey to its mouth.

Fact The second-largest cuttlefish species, the broadclub dazzles its prey by changing its color and emitting waves of light. To avoid capture, it releases ink.

Conservation status   **Not evaluated**

Southern Blue-ringed Octopus

Hapalochlaena maculosa

Ocean animals

Invertebrates

Mollusks

Factfile

Habitat	Coastal waters, tide pools, reefs
Distribution	Southern Australia
Size	2 in. (body), 4 in. (arms)
Weight	Up to 13.5 oz.
Life span	Up to 2 years
Predators	Sharks, moray eels, large fish

Diet The blue-ringed octopus wounds its prey of crustaceans and small fish with its beak, and injects a venom that stuns and quickly kills its victim.

Fact When threatened, iridescent blue rings develop on its body and arms. It is not aggressive, but its venom is one of the most deadly, even to humans.

Conservation status   Not evaluated

Dumbo Octopus
Grimpoteuthis

Factfile

Habitat	Deep tropical to temperate waters
Distribution	Worldwide
Length	8 to 12 in.
Weight	Not recorded
Life span	3 to 5 years
Predators	Sharks, orcas, tuna

Diet Moving just above the seabed, their fins flapping, dumbo octopuses pounce on their invertebrate prey, trap it in their arms and eat it whole.

Fact The ear-like fins on these octopuses earned them the "Dumbo" nickname. They are the deepest-living octopuses, surviving cold water and no sunlight.

Conservation status   **Not evaluated**

Striped P jama Squid

Sepioloidea lineolata

Factfile

Habitat	Coastal shallow seabeds
Distribution	Eastern and southern Australian coasts
Length	2 in. (mantle only)
Weight	Not recorded
Life span	3 to 10 months
Predators	Few natural predators (adults)

Diet The striped pyjama squid eats shrimp and fish. During the day, it ambushes prey by burying itself with only its eyes protruding. At night, it hunts for prey.

Fact The black-and-white stripes of this squid (actually a cuttlefish) warn predators that its mucus is toxic. It is one of only three venomous cephalopods.

Conservation status   Not evaluated

Chambered Nautilus

Nautilus pompilius

Factfile

Habitat	Tropical waters
Distribution	Western Pacific Ocean
Length	8 to 10 in.
Weight	2 lb. (shell and body)
Life span	Up to 20 years
Predators	Octopuses, sharks, triggerfish, turtles

Diet The chambered nautilus scavenges in shallow waters at night for hermit crabs, fish, carrion and the discarded shells of molting crustaceans.

Fact Nautilus were around 265 million years before the dinosaurs. They are living fossils, as they have not changed in 400 million years.

Conservation status   **Not evaluated**

Queen Conch

Strombus gigas

Factfile

Habitat	Sandy and seagrass beds, coral reefs
Distribution	Caribbean Sea, Gulf of Mexico
Length	12 in.
Weight	5 lb.
Life span	20 to 30 years
Predators	Sea snails, starfish, fish, sea turtles, humans

Diet The queen conch lives on seabeds, grazing on algae and detritus. Two pairs of tentacles provide sight, smell and touch. It eats through its extendable "nose."

Fact The spiral shell of the queen conch protects the soft-bodied mollusk inhabitant. It is overfished, as the shell and meat have commercial value.

Conservation status   Not evaluated

Triton's Trumpet Snail

Charonia tritonis

Factfile

Habitat	Tropical coral reefs, sand flats
Distribution	Indo-Pacific Ocean, Red Sea
Width	23.5 in.
Weight	Not recorded
Life span	Not recorded
Predators	No natural predators, humans

Diet This triton will chase its prey of sea stars and other snails. Its venomous saliva subdues the prey, and then it bores into the sea star to access the meat.

Fact Triton's trumpet, so-named as the shell makes a noise when blown, is one of only a few predators of the reef-killing crown-of-thorns starfish.

Conservation status   **Not evaluated**

Flamingo Tongue Snail

Cyphoma gibbosum

Factfile

Habitat	Shallow tropical reefs
Distribution	Southwestern Atlantic Ocean
Length	1 to 1.5 in.
Weight	Not reported
Life span	Up to 2 years
Predators	Hogfish, pufferfish, Caribbean spiny lobsters

Diet This marine snail preys on soft corals, especially sea fans and whip corals. It eats the soft tissue, leaving the coral's skeleton behind.

Fact The shell of the flamingo tongue is white. It is the soft body inside that is colorfully patterned, which warns prey that it tastes unpleasant.

Conservation status   **Not evaluated**

Spanish Dancer

Hexabranchus sanguineus

Factfile

Habitat	Tropical coral and rocky reefs
Distribution	Western Pacific and Indian Oceans
Length	Up to 10 in.
Weight	Not reported
Life span	1 year
Predators	Emperor shrimp

Diet Spanish dancers eat sponges and jellyfish, and utilize the chemical compounds from their prey to make their own chemically toxic defenses.

Fact This is the largest of the nudibranch and one of the largest sea slugs. It only leaves the seabed, mantle unfurled and gills flapping, when threatened.

Conservation status   **Not evaluated**

Common Limpet

Patella vulgata

Ocean animals

Invertebrates

Mollusks

Factfile

Habitat	Rock shelves along seashores
Distribution	Arctic Circle to Portugal
Length	Up to 3 in. (shell)
Weight	.5 to 1.4 oz.
Life span	Up to 16 years
Predators	Starfish, seabirds, fish, seals, humans

Diet Limpets graze on microscopic algae, scraping it off the rocks with their toothed file-like "tongue." The teeth are strengthened with iron.

Fact Limpets nearer the shoreline have taller domed shells than those farther from shore. After feeding they return to their original anchor spot.

Conservation status   **Not evaluated**

Giant Clam

Tridacna gigas

Factfile

Habitat	Warm waters
Distribution	South Pacific and Indian Oceans
Length	4 ft.
Weight	500 lb.
Life span	100 years or more
Predators	Eels, snails, starfish

Diet Once a clam selects a site, it remains there, filtering water via a siphon to extract plankton. It also consumes sugars produced by the algae in its tissues.

Fact The giant clam is the largest mollusk on the planet. It was once thought to be a man-eater, but the muscles that close the shell react very slowly.

Conservation status   **Vulnerable**

Pacific Oyster

Crassostrea gigas

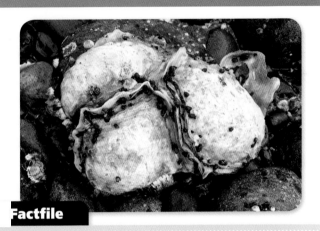

Factfile

Habitat	Hard tidal and estuary surfaces
Distribution	Native to Japan, now cultivated worldwide
Length	Up to 12 in.
Weight	2.5 to 3.5 oz. (including shell)
Life span	Up to 20 years (in captivity)
Predators	Crabs, oyster drills, starfish

Diet Once the larvae have chosen an anchoring spot, the oyster will not move. It feeds by filtering plankton and detritus from the water that passes over it.

Fact Once only found in Japan, the Pacific oyster has been introduced into many countries and is farmed because its meat is prized as a food source.

Conservation status   **Not evaluated**

106

Antarctic Krill
Euphausia superba

Factfile

Habitat	Cold open oceans
Distribution	Antarctica
Length	Up to 2.5 in.
Weight	Up to .1 oz.
Life span	6 to 10 years
Predators	Adélie penguins, fish, birds, seals, whales

Diet Antarctic krill consume single-celled plants (plankton) that drift near the ocean's surface. They can go without food for up to 200 days.

Fact These crustaceans mass in schools so enormous that they can be seen from space. They are an important source of food for hundreds of species.

Conservation status   **Least concern**

Peacock Mantis Shrimp

Odontodactylus scyllarus

Ocean animals

Invertebrates

Crustaceans

Factfile

Habitat	Tropical sandy reef seabeds
Distribution	Indian and Pacific Oceans
Length	1.2 to 7 in.
Weight	Not reported
Life span	4 to 6 years
Predators	Yellowfin tuna, large reef fish (young only)

Diet This seabed animal uses its club-like appendages to punch its prey. The punch can crack the shells of invertebrates and even aquarium glass.

Fact Named for its brilliant coloring, this shrimp's complex eyes have sixteen color receptors to track prey and avoid predators.

Conservation status   Not evaluated

Caribbean Spiny Lobster

Panulirus argus

Factfile

Habitat	Rocky and coral reefs, seagrass beds
Distribution	Caribbean Sea, Gulf of Mexico
Length	Up to 18 in.
Weight	Up to 20 lb.
Life span	12 to 20 years
Predators	Grouper, sharks, loggerhead turtles, octopuses

Diet At night this lobster, an opportunistic feeder, leaves its daytime crevices to forage for slow-moving prey, like snails and crabs, and detritus.

Fact Like all decapods, the hard shell is the lobster's skeleton. As it does not expand, it must shed it to reveal the new skeleton developing below.

Conservation status   **Not evaluated**

European Lobster

Homarus gammarus

Ocean animals

Invertebrates

Crustaceans

Factfile

Habitat	Coastal temperate waters
Distribution	Northeastern Atlantic Ocean
Length	Up to 3.2 ft.
Weight	Up to 20 lb.
Life span	Over 15 years
Predators	Cod, eels, flatfish, crabs, lobsters (young only)

Diet This lobster is a nocturnal scavenger of mussels, hermit crabs, sea urchins and worms. One pincer crushes prey, while the other holds and tears it.

Fact In their natural environment, European lobsters are blue. They turn red when cooked. They are a highly prized and valuable seafood.

Conservation status   **Least concern**

Atlantic Blue Crab

Callinectes sapidus

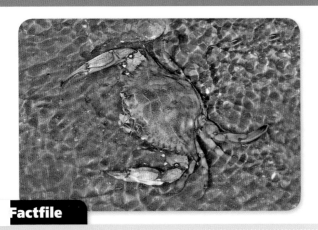

Factfile

Habitat	Soft-bottomed estuaries and shallow waters
Distribution	Eastern Atlantic Ocean
Width	Up to 9 in. (carapace only)
Weight	1 to 2 lb.
Life span	3 years
Predators	Other blue crabs, eels, striped bass, and more

Diet
The Atlantic blue crab is an omnivore that will eat anything, dead or alive, including snails, fish, seagrass, smaller blue crabs, bivalves and shrimp.

Fact
When the blue crab molts, the new skeleton is initially soft. When commercially fished at this stage, they are sold as soft-shell crabs.

Conservation status   **Not evaluated**

Red King Crab

Paralithodes camtschaticus

Ocean animals

Invertebrates

Crustaceans

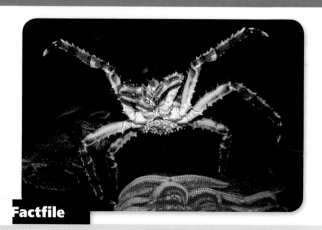

Factfile

Habitat	Coastal temperate waters, polar waters
Distribution	Northern Pacific Ocean
Length	6 ft. (including leg span)
Weight	Up to 22 lb.
Life span	15 to 20 years
Predators	Other king crabs, sea otters, sculpins, octopuses

Diet This omnivore crab includes fish, mollusks, worms, crustaceans, algae, sponges, echinoderms, carrion and plankton in its wide diet.

Fact Adult red king crabs have few predators because their shell is thick and armored with spikes. Juveniles mass in huge clusters to avoid predators.

Conservation status   **Not evaluated**

Atlantic Horseshoe Crab

Limulus polyphemus

Factfile

Habitat	Muddy and sandy estuaries and bays
Distribution	Northwestern Atlantic Ocean
Length	Up to 2 ft.
Weight	Up to 11 ft.
Life span	19 years
Predators	Sharks, turtles (adults), seabirds (young only)

Diet Horseshoe crabs dig for worms, mollusks, algae and carrion. The food is crushed by bristles on its legs as it walks, then pushed towards its mouth.

Fact A component of this crab's copper-based blue blood is used to test the safety of vaccines and intravenous drugs, and the sterility of medical equipment.

Conservation status   **Not evaluated**

113

Crown-of-thorns Starfish

Acanthaster planci

Ocean animals

Invertebrates

Echinoderms

Factfile

Habitat	Tropical ocean reefs
Distribution	Pacific and Indian Oceans
Width	10 to 14 in.
Weight	Up to 6.5 lb.
Life span	Up to 4 years
Predators	Guard crabs, tritons, Maori wrasses

Diet This starfish feeds on hard corals. It pushes its stomach out through its mouth, covers the coral and liquefies the tissue, and consumes the nutrients.

Fact The crown-of-thorns starfish can regenerate broken spines and arms, even if only half the body remains. Its spines are venomous.

Conservation status   Not evaluated

Cushion Star

Culcita novaeguineae

Factfile

Habitat	Tropical ocean coral reefs
Distribution	Central and western Pacific and Indian Oceans
Width	Up to 12 in.
Weight	2.2 to 6 lb.
Life span	Unknown
Predators	Other sea stars, tritons, crabs, fish, otters, birds

Diet Cushion stars feed on corals and small sedentary (inactive) invertebrates. They obtain nutrients in the same way as the crown-of-thorns starfish.

Fact As juveniles, cushion stars resemble other sea stars, but as they grow larger they balloon and the arms grow together to resemble five-sided pincushions.

Conservation status   **Not evaluated**

Eccentric Sand Dollar

Dendraster excentricus

Ocean animals

Invertebrates

Echinoderms

Factfile

Habitat	Sandy coastal seabeds
Distribution	Northeastern Pacific Ocean
Width	Up to 4 in.
Weight	Not recorded
Life span	Up to 13 years
Predators	No natural predators

Diet Sand dollars lie half buried on sandy seabeds while hairs on their surface carry minute bits of organic matter to their mouth on the underside.

Fact Sand dollars are flattened relatives of sea urchins. Little more than skeletons, they move on sand using tiny spines rather than their tube feet.

Conservation status   Not evaluated

Edible Sea Cucumber

Holothuria edulis

Factfile

Habitat   Tropical sandy reefs, seagrass beds
Distribution Indian and Pacific Oceans
Length   8 to 12 in.
Weight   7 to 10.5 oz.
Life span   5 to 10 years
Predators   Crabs, fish, crustaceans, sea stars, turtles, humans

Diet This sea cucumber crawls over seabeds, eating sand and mud from which organic matter is digested. The cleaned sand is passed out through the anus.

Fact As a food source, this animal is called *bêche-de-mer*, which means "sea spade." A sea cucumber can process several tons of sand a year.

Conservation status   **Least concern**

Sea Wasp

Chironex fleckeri

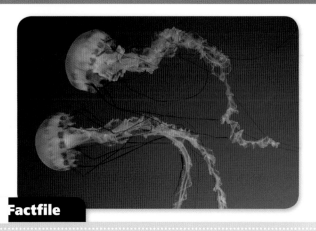

Factfile

Habitat	Tropical coastal waters
Distribution	Southwestern Pacific Ocean
Size	10 ft. (tentacles), 10 in. (bell width)
Weight	Up to 4.5 lb.
Life span	Less than 1 year
Predators	Leatherback turtles

Diet The sea wasp hunts fish, swimming crabs and prawns and snares them in its tentacles that trail ten feet behind it. The prey dies instantly.

Fact The venom of the sea wasp can kill up to sixty people, and can cause death in three minutes. There are 5,000 stinging cells on its sixty tentacles.

Conservation status   **Not evaluated**

Moon Jellyfish

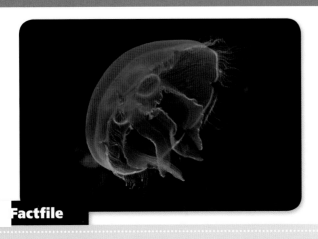

Factfile

Habitat	Brackish waters to open oceans, near the surface
Distribution	Atlantic, Pacific and Indian Oceans
Size	10 to 16 in.
Weight	Not recorded
Life span	6 months
Predators	Sunfish, sea turtles, seabirds, tuna, spiny dogfish

Diet This jellyfish drift feeds on mollusks, crustaceans and worms that get caught in its mucus coating. Tiny hairs move the food to its mouth.

Fact These jellyfish do not have a brain and their body is ninety-five percent water. They have minimal locomotion, so rely on currents and winds to carry them.

Conservation status   Not evaluated

Lion's Mane Jellyfish

Cyanea capillata

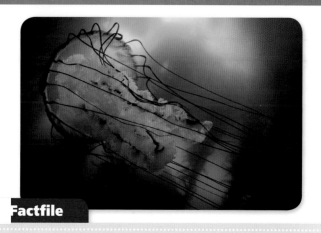

Factfile

Habitat	Cooler open oceans
Distribution	North Atlantic and Pacific Oceans, North Sea
Size	100 ft. (tentacles), 6.5 ft. (bell width)
Weight	Up to 500 lb.
Life span	1 year
Predators	Ocean sunfish, sea turtles, seabirds

Diet Lion's mane jellyfish have about 1,200 tentacles covered with stinging cells to kill their preferred prey of zooplankton, small fish and other jellyfish.

Fact These giants of the jellyfish world form schools half a mile wide and can produce their own light. They can swim, but also use currents and wind.

Conservation status   Not evaluated

Portuguese Man o' War

Physalia physalis

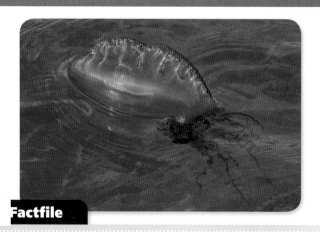

Factfile

Habitat	Tropical coasts, on the water surface
Distribution	Worldwide
Size	Up to 165 ft., (tentacles), up to 12 in. (float)
Weight	Not recorded
Life span	Up to 1 year
Predators	Fish, crustaceans

Diet The man o' war's tentacles contain stinging cells that can paralyze and kill fish and crustaceans. The food is then moved to the colony's feeding polyps.

Fact The man o' war is a colony of four types of polyps. Each polyp performs a different function: floating, feeding, capturing prey or reproduction.

Conservation status   Not evaluated

Elkhorn Coral

Acropora palmata

Ocean animals

Invertebrates

Corals

Factfile

Habitat	Heavy wave areas in coral reefs
Distribution	Western Atlantic Ocean, Caribbean Sea
Size	Up to 10 ft. (diameter)
Weight	Not recorded
Life span	5 to 1,000s of years (colony), 2 to 3 years (polyps)
Predators	Bearded fireworm snails, damselfish, humans

Diet Zooxanthellae, an algae, live in the coral's tissues and make food for the coral using photosynthesis. It is the algae that give the coral its colors.

Fact The fast-growing elkhorn is an important reef-building coral. Colonies are endangered due to climate change, storms and disease.

Conservation status   Critically endangered

Giant Caribbean Sea Anemone

Condylactis gigantea

Factfile

Habitat	Inshore coral reef waters
Distribution	Caribbean Sea, Gulf of Mexico
Size	6 in. (high), 12 in. (wide)
Weight	Not recorded
Life span	12 to 25 years
Predators	Red-leg hermit crabs

Diet This anemone can move, but when "hunting" it remains still, letting its tentacles sting and transport fish, mussels and shrimp to its mouth.

Fact When threatened, this anemone draws its 100 or so tentacles into its stomach so as to reduce its size. Its defense is its toxin-loaded tentacle tips.

Conservation status   Not evaluated

Yellow Tube Sponge

Aplysina insularis

Ocean animals

Invertebrates

Sponges

Factfile

Habitat	Coral and rocky reefs in open waters
Distribution	Western Atlantic Ocean, Gulf of Mexico
Height	Up to 4 ft.
Weight	Not recorded
Life span	Possibly to 100 years (unconfirmed)
Predators	Hawksbill turtles, reef fishes

Diet Yellow tube sponges are fixed to the seabed, so they feed by extracting organic particles from the water that flows through the tube walls.

Fact The cells that make up a sponge can transform to perform any function. If a sponge is pulped in a blender, the cells regroup to reform the sponge.

Conservation status	Not evaluated

Divided Flatworm
Pseudoceros dimidiatus

Factfile

Habitat	Tropical coral and rocky reefs
Distribution	Indian and Pacific Oceans
Length	3 in.
Weight	Not recorded
Life span	65 to 140 days (in captivity)
Predators	Crustaceans, fish (adults)

Diet Flatworms lie on their prey – worms and snails – and insert a tube that grinds up the prey and acts as a straw through which to suck the meal.

Fact Divided flatworms move quickly on millions of pulsating hairs. Their body colors vary, but all warn predators that they make nasty eating.

Conservation status   **Not evaluated**

Glossary

Algae Aquatic plants and single-celled organisms.

Ambush predator An animal that hides and waits for prey.

Annelid A ringed or segmented worm.

Arthropod An invertebrate with an external skeleton, segmented body and joined limbs.

Baleen plate A structure in a whale's mouth that strains food.

Bivalve A mollusk that has a pair of hinged shells.

Bony fish Fish with a skeleton of bone rather than cartilage.

Brackish Slightly salty water.

Carapace Hard upper shell of an animal.

Carcass Dead body of an animal.

Carnivore An animal that feeds on other animals.

Carrion Decaying flesh of dead animals.

Cephalopod A type of mollusk including octopuses, squid, cuttlefish and nautilus.

Cnidaria Aquatic animal including jellyfish, corals and anemones.

Coastal A region of water that meets land.

Coral polyp A soft-bodied organism with a limestone skeleton that divides to build coral reefs.

Crustacean A type of arthropod such as crabs, lobsters and krill.

Decapod A crustacean, like a shrimp or crab, which has ten legs.

Detritus Matter produced by decaying organisms.

Drift feeder An animal that feeds on invertebrates that drift on the water surface.

Echinoderm An animal, like a starfish, with five-point symmetry.

Estuary Where tidal water meets a river.

Excreta Waste that is expelled from the body.

Filter feeding Process of filtering water to extract food.

Forage To search far for food.

Gastropod A type of mollusk including snails, slugs and limpets.

Herbivore An animal that feeds on plants.

Ice floe A sheet of floating ice.

Inshore Area of water close to the shore.

Intertidal Land covered at high tide and uncovered at low tide.

Invertebrate An animal without a backbone including crabs, snails and octopuses.

Juvenile A young animal.

Kelp A brown seaweed.

Keystone species An animal that has a unique role in an ecosystem.

Lagoon A body of saltwater separated from the sea by a sandbank or reef.

Larva The young of an animal.

Mangrove A small tree growing in salty or brackish water.

Mollusk A soft-bodied animal without a backbone, including snails, mussels and squid.

Nudibranch A soft-bodied, strikingly colored type of mollusk, like a sea slug.

Omnivore An animal that eats both meat and plants.

Opportunistic An animal that exploits any food options.

Organic Anything that has come from a living creature.

Parasite A plant or animal that benefits from another living thing.

Photophores A light-producing organ.

Photosynthesis Using sunlight to make nutrients and oxygen from carbon dioxide and water.

Plankton Small or microscopic organisms.

Proboscis A nose, especially a long one like a trunk.

Reef A ridge of rock, coral or sand above or below the sea.

Scavenger An animal that feeds on dead material and garbage.

School (or shoal) A large group of sea animals.

Seagrass A grasslike plant that grows in or near the sea.

Semiaquatic Being able to live on land and in water.

Shellfish Marine animals with a shell or exoskeleton.

Spawning When an animal releases its eggs.

Sponge An animal that filter feeds via holes in its body.

Temperate A body of water with mild temperatures.

Territorial An animal that remains in and defends its "home."

Tropical Constantly warm water found between the tropics of Cancer and Capricorn.

Tunicate An invertebrate filter feeder like a sea squirt.

Vertebrate A mammal, bird, reptile, amphibian or fish with a backbone.

Zooplankton Tiny and juvenile plankton that drift on currents.

Index